Blue Peter

Blue Peter

54

42

Written by
Steve Hocking,
Anne Dixon and
Bridget Caldwell

14

38

30

CONTENTS

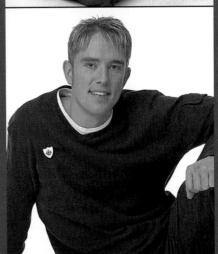

Konnie Huq

Simon Thomas

Matt Baker

Liz Barker

Lucy

Mabel

Meg

Top: Kari and Oke sat still long enough to be captured on canvas.
Above: Simon investigated the history of Highland dress and met up with a Scottish Scout pack.
Below: K-9 the robot dog helped inspire over 32,000 viewers to send us robot designs of their own.

Two important homes: Above, Osborne House on the Isle of Wight was Queen Victoria's favourite home. Right: We helped build a new wildlife pond at the Prime Minister's home, 10 Downing Street.

HELLO there!

Konnie (above) drove for glory in a World Rally Championship event in Sweden while Simon (below) scaled the Humber Bridge – don't look down!

Welcome to the latest **Blue Peter book.** It's been a great year for all of us on Blue Peter and we hope that you'll find some of your favourite moments on the pages that follow. You can travel the world from Spain to San Francisco, from La Palma to Peru. Go star-spotting with Konnie on a Spanish island, travel back to the glories of Rome with Simon; see Matt and Mabel turned into Vikings and Liz becoming a firefighter. As always, we've got tricks to learn and loads of ideas for things to make and do. You can find out what happens when Blue Peter leaves the studio for a live show on the road and pick up ideas for great days out that you could enjoy with a Blue Peter badge. **This is the thirty first Blue Peter book and we hope you enjoy it.**

Above: At the Kilmore and Kilbride Highland Games Simon and Matt tried everything from caber tossing to tug of war.
Below: All dressed up for a Christmas Cockney knees-up.

7

Snaps from
SAN FRANCISCO

One of the best things about being a Blue Peter presenter is the chance to travel the world. This year has taken the team all over the globe, but one of the most exciting trips was Simon and Matt's trip to the west coast of the USA ... to San Francisco!

MATT: "What a view! The Golden Gate Bridge. We'd just arrived when this photo was taken, and the weather was glorious. We were making several films and I wore a different shirt for each one. As it takes several days to shoot each story you have to take a couple of identical shirts with you ... there's never enough time to catch up with the washing!"

SIMON: "I don't usually drive a car like this, but I wouldn't have minded bringing this one back home! We hired a convertible car for a couple of hours to film the opening sequence of our film from the city. How cool was that?!"

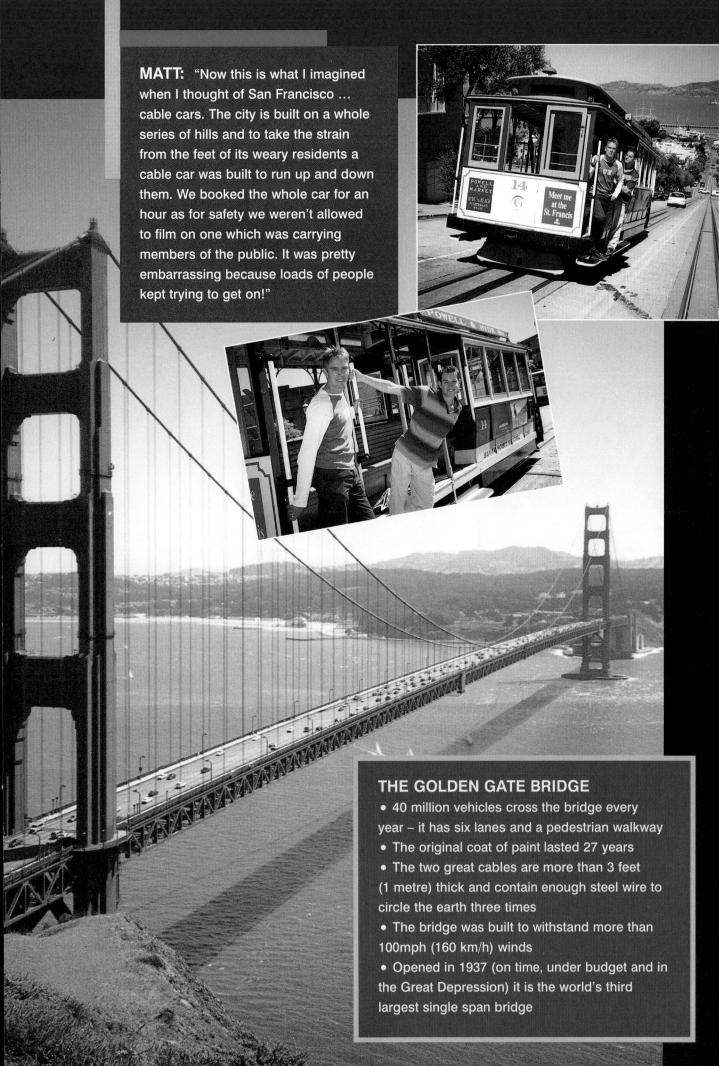

MATT: "Now this is what I imagined when I thought of San Francisco … cable cars. The city is built on a whole series of hills and to take the strain from the feet of its weary residents a cable car was built to run up and down them. We booked the whole car for an hour as for safety we weren't allowed to film on one which was carrying members of the public. It was pretty embarrassing because loads of people kept trying to get on!"

THE GOLDEN GATE BRIDGE

• 40 million vehicles cross the bridge every year – it has six lanes and a pedestrian walkway
• The original coat of paint lasted 27 years
• The two great cables are more than 3 feet (1 metre) thick and contain enough steel wire to circle the earth three times
• The bridge was built to withstand more than 100mph (160 km/h) winds
• Opened in 1937 (on time, under budget and in the Great Depression) it is the world's third largest single span bridge

SIMON: "The strangest report was from a bathtub, where my jeans were being shrunk to fit me better! San Francisco was the home of Levi Strauss, whose denim jeans are famous all over the world. Today you can have your body scanned to produce measurements so precise that your tailor-made jeans fit perfectly … after a good soaking. They fitted though!"

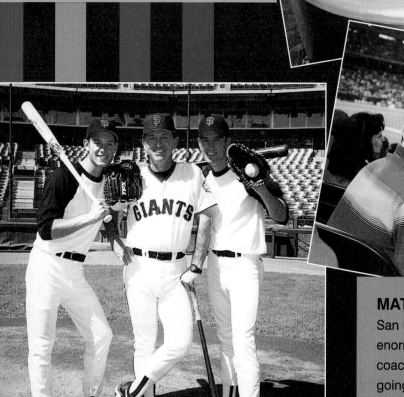

MATT: "Baseball is huge in America. The San Francisco Giants have just moved to an enormous new stadium and we met one of their coaches, Carlos Alfonso. I can't say that he was going to sign us for the team, but we had great fun and learned a lot. He seemed impressed with our efforts!"

BASEBALL
• The World Series was first held in 1903. It takes place each October and is the best of seven matches
• Professional baseball's most important event is the end of season game between the winners of the two major baseball leagues in the USA – the National League and the American League

SIMON: "When I visited Alcatraz, the prison built on an island in the middle of San Francisco Bay, the weather was as grey as the building. Alcatraz is a big tourist attraction today, but once it was home to some of the most feared criminals in the USA. It's a grim place. No one ever escaped from behind these bars."

ALCATRAZ

- The maximum security prison on Alcatraz, called 'the Rock', housed an average of 264 of America's most dangerous criminals
- Prisoners spent between 16 and 23 hours a day confined to their cells
- Alcatraz means 'pelican' in Spanish
- The only means of escape was across 3 miles of freezing treacherous water

SIMON: "The giant redwoods in Muir Woods (just outside San Francisco) are anything up to 1,000 years old. The tallest coast redwood in the US is in California's Prairie Creek Redwoods State Park and is an incredible 95.4 metres high."

★ KONNIE

Now you see it Now you don't!

Normally magicians are sworn to secrecy on how their tricks are done but Konnie has been given special permission to show you how to perform the first trick she ever learnt – how to make a coin magically disappear in front of your friends' eyes!

THE TRICK

Ladies and gentlemen, does anyone have a coin I could borrow?

Now, by the power of magic, I will make your coin disappear before your very eyes. I have here an ordinary glass and a handkerchief.

I put the cloth over the glass and then place the glass over the coin. Say the magic words – 'Blue Peter' – and, hey presto, the coin has disappeared into thin air!

TO FIND OUT HOW KONNIE MADE THE COIN DISAPPEAR TURN TO PAGE 45

MATT'S BEST FRIEND

This is me!

Blue Peter

Moving south was a big hurdle for Matt, but after a year he realised the one thing he missed more than anything was a dog. Never one to waste time, he sent word to his sheep dog training pal, Derek, to see if he knew of any expected Border Collie litters of puppies.

Matt's always been surrounded by Border Collies working on the Baker farm. They are a highly intelligent working breed and that was what he wanted – a clever dog to be his constant companion.

Matt was in luck. A neighbour's dog was due to give birth in December and Matt was promised the pick of the litter. On 6 December 2000 the news came that nine puppies had been born and all were gorgeous. So it was off to Weardale at the first opportunity to see which little bundle of fur made Matt's knees go weakest. What a decision! Matt knew he wanted a girl with traditional markings and a good temperament. "There she was looking right at me! She was an absolute beauty," said Matt. The pup stayed with her mum and the rest of the pups until she was eleven weeks old and had had all her preliminary inoculations.

The countdown to the day when the little black and white dog would come to the studio had begun. Matt brought his pup to have a look around Television Centre a few days before her first appearance. She was a natural, who loved everybody and everything.

The big day – Monday 19 February 2001. Apart from the millions of Blue Peter viewers, who better to show her off to than vet Joe Ingles. (Joe is another fan of Border Collies and thought Matt's pup was adorable.)

14

Joe gave her an injection to ensure she wouldn't catch any of the five major diseases – the worst ones being parvo virus and distemper. Joe said that after another week she'd be ready to face the big outdoors. The other thing she needed was a name. Matt had been mulling over loads of ideas. It had to be short and sweet – and he chose the name Meg.

Meg gets on well with Mabel, Lucy, Kari and Oke and has already mastered several important commands. She is growing fast, so keep watching for more tales of Matt and Meg…

Blue Peter
STAMP AID 2000

Top left: After just two weeks our Liverpool depot had received 9 million stamps.
Top right: The 6th Forfar Brownies sent us a huge donation of 11,942 stamps.

Health Unlimited is a small charity that runs projects in many parts of the world providing health care. We wanted to help their work in Peru where they train local people to be health workers themselves. That was why Simon found himself climbing the mountains of the Peruvian Andes to help launch the Stamp Aid Appeal, our 39th.

The Andes are among the highest mountains in the world and the Quechua people who live in the high valleys are a long way from the modern facilities available to most of the people of Peru. There isn't a chemist on the corner, let alone a doctor or a hospital. Even basic health care is many hours', even days', journey away. Simon met many children and their families who would benefit from better health care. Complaints like toothache and diarrhoea can become life threatening if not treated quickly.

Simon visited some villages where Health Unlimited had provided Qampi Wasis, or health posts, and saw what a difference they made. Sadly not all villages were as lucky.

How could we help? We wanted to collect something that everyone has plenty of at Christmas – stamps! The Post Office told us that 200 stamps could be posted to our Stamp Aid Depot for the price of a second class stamp. We worked out that we'd need millions of stamps to fund the work in Peru.

Our first target was 100,000 envelopes to pay for Qampi Wasis to be built in three remote villages. By the end of March we reckoned that you had sent approaching a million envelopes – roughly 187 million stamps. Thanks to your efforts 21 communities will be helped. Your postage stamps have been sold and will pay for building and equipping health posts plus training local people to be health workers and birth attendants. The Stamp Aid Appeal has also provided 32 mountain bikes for workers who need them plus a vehicle and driver to help the Health Unlimited team in Peru with their life saving work.

A big THANK YOU to everyone who worked so hard to provide long lasting health care for children and their families living high up in the Andes.

In the village of Wachgaga Simon met some of the children your stamps will help.

The top of our totaliser was soon flashing 100,000 – and your envelopes just kept coming.

100 000
90 000
70 000
50 000
30 000
20 000
15 000
10 000
5 000
1 000

Stamp Aid

Simon travelled across the Andes seeing for himself the Qampi Wasis we plan to build and the villages that need them.

Hola! This is us in the Plaza de Espana in Seville – the starting place for our journey across Andalusia.

BLUE PETER SUMMER EXPEDITION 2000

VIVA ESPANA!

The destination for the 2000 Summer Expedition was SPAIN. Over 10 million Brits go there every year but, as we found on our travels, it has a lot more to offer than sun, sea and sand.

Left: Matt outside Casa Mila in Barcelona – one of Antonio Gaudi's most famous houses.
Right: Debbie (the PA) relaxes in one of Madrid's squares dressed as a bear!

18

MADRID

The capital of Spain is Madrid, Europe's highest capital city. It's here that we tried some typical Spanish food — **tapas.** They're small snacks and there's loads to choose from, ranging from olives and cheese to garlic prawns, spicy sausage and octopus. The idea dates from the nineteenth century when bartenders would keep flies out of drinks by covering the glass with a lid or tapa. This would sometimes be a piece of bread and gradually tasty titbits were put on top – and the rest, as they say, is history.

We also went filming in the **Parque del Retro,** Madrid's most popular park. Simon was chased through the park by a group of Tunas (modern day Spanish wandering minstrels), Konnie played Kayak water polo and Debbie (the Production Assistant) dressed up as a bear – all the things you'd expect on a typical Blue Peter filming day.

Top left: Konnie is serenaded by a group of wandering minstrels.
Above: Liz by the Roman Aqueduct in Segovia.

Above: Simon meets some young fans of Real Madrid football team.

Left: Buen apetito! Here we are in Madrid tucking into some tasty tapas.

19

Mind your heads! Konnie and Simon have a go at harvesting almonds in Majorca.

BARCELONA

Spain is made up of 17 different regions, some of which have their own language. For example in the **Basque Country** in Northern Spain they speak Euskadi and when we visited the capital of the **Catalonian** region, Barcelona, we met people who spoke Catalan. It's one of Spain's most stylish cities full of amazing art and architecture. Matt checked out buildings by the architect **Antonio Gaudi,** including his Casa Mila which is pretty unusual looking as there are no straight walls anywhere.

SEGOVIA

The next day we had a day trip to Segovia, which is where you find one of the largest Roman constructions still standing in Spain. It's an **aqueduct** made up of 163 arches and is 800 metres long and 29 metres high. The most amazing thing about it is that not a single drop of mortar or cement was used to hold it together – just good old Roman know-how! We missed our turning on our journey back to Madrid and ended up travelling through the mountains on very windy roads. It was very pretty but we had a bit of a shock when we drove around a corner and came face to face with three wild bulls!

Spanish children training to be matadors in Seville.

DON QUIXOTE

When we told one of Spain's best known stories, 'Don Quixote', Simon dressed up as the Don while Liz was Sancho, his friend. She had to stuff a pillow up her shirt because Sancho is meant to be pot-bellied! In part of the story Don Quixote asks someone to knight him, but the man refuses, thinking the Don is mad. We asked a local man to help us re-enact this scene – we think he thought we were as mad as Don Quixote.

Right: Ready for action – Simon and Liz dress up as Don Quixote and Sancho. Left: Simon asks a local man to knight him.

20

MAJORCA

As well as exploring mainland Spain, we also visited some of the country's islands including Majorca. It's said to produce the best **almonds** in the world. Two local farmers were harvesting some of the nuts in the traditional way. They didn't speak much English, but Simon and Konnie offered to give them a hand, and it soon became obvious what had to be done. The trick is to hit the almond tree branches with long sticks so the nuts fall to the ground. Simon got really into it – he hit one branch with so much force that he broke his stick!

ANDALUSIA

Andalusia, in the sunny south, is where you find everything that's typically Spanish. The capital of the region is **Seville** and it's here that Konnie visited a bullfighting school. Whatever your feelings are about this, it is still popular in Spain. And it's big business, with bullfighters earning as much as pop stars and footballers. At the school Konnie saw children as young as seven training to be matadors. Spain's oldest bullring can be found in the small town of **Ronda** which is also where Matt had a lesson in flamenco dancing. He was lent a traditional costume which was a bit too small for him, so he was frightened about bending over just in case his trousers split!

Above: Flamenco is quite tricky but Matt picked it up really quickly and impressed the other dancers with his nifty footwork.

Simon and Liz charge at windmills – no, they're not mad, just re-enacting a famous scene from Don Quixote.

Up, up and away. Konnie takes to the skies in a hot air balloon for a bird's eye view of Ronda.

21

On the way to Spain's most southern tip we stopped off to film some windmills. We were heading for **Tarifa,** which gets incredibly windy and makes it a perfect place for windsurfing. Simon was meeting the Andalusian windsurfing champion, Carlos Van de Loox, who gave him a few tips. And after falling off a few times, it wasn't long before Simon got the hang of it.

One of Konnie's highlights was taking to the skies in a hot air balloon. It was fantastic – one moment you're on the ground and then suddenly you find yourself up in the air. It was so peaceful floating through the skies looking at the Spanish countryside.

Andalusia is also famous for its beaches, and at **Nerja** Liz had a cookery lesson with a Spanish chef called Ayo. He's famous for the giant paellas he cooks on the beach. It was hot work. Ayo used a rake to move the pan round the open fire. "It's a bit like gardening!" Liz commented. It took about an hour to cook and when it was ready Liz dished some up for the others. And the verdict? Delicious!

No, Matt didn't forget his trunks. The reason he's in caving gear is that he's about to go filming in Nerja's famous caves.

ALMERIA

Next destination was Almeria, which is where you find Europe's only desert. It's one of the driest parts of Europe and, as you'd expect, they get a lot of sunshine. Because of its wild and rocky scenery Almeria was chosen as the place to film some of Hollywood's most famous Westerns of all time – the **Spaghetti Westerns**. Once filming was over, they left behind three wild west town sets including one at Mini Hollywood, and here we recreated our own Spaghetti Western with Simon as the Sheriff and Matt as the Champion Kid. Matt kept getting the giggles every time Simon spoke in a slow American drawl – not very Clint Eastwood.

Howdy, partners – this is us dressed up for our spaghetti western.

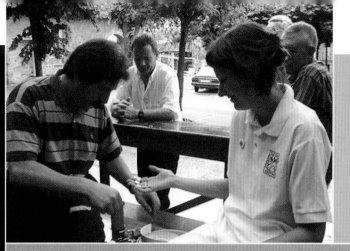

PICOS D'EUROPA

We visited a massive mountain range in Northern Spain – the **Picos D'Europa.** The mountains were very beautiful and, compared to the rest of Spain, very green. But we hadn't just come here for the scenery – Simon and Liz were going to try paragliding. This was Liz's first big Blue Peter challenge, and even though she doesn't like heights she really went for it. Both presenters had a special small digital camera strapped to their wrist so they could give a running commentary on what it was like as they were gliding through the air.

BASQUE COUNTRY

In the Basque Country Liz was introduced to one of the region's sports, **Pelota.** It's a bit like the game of squash where you hit a very hard ball against a wall but instead of using a racquet you use your hand, which is bound up. Not many women play the game, but the locals really enjoyed seeing Liz have a go. In fact they even gave her a standing ovation! The next day, however, her hand really ached.

FIESTA!

Spanish people really know how to party. On our last day we went to a fiesta in the village of Villa Nova where they celebrate by building a **castaller,** or human tower. Everyone in the village takes part. The aim is to make the tallest tower and the villagers of Villa Nova were competing against two other villages. Matt got the chance to have a go, joining in to make up a tower. He was one of the bases and he had people climbing up on top to make the tower higher and higher. He really had to concentrate so that the people on top of him didn't fall. And then it was time to join in with the rest of the fiesta with music, dancing and fireworks – a perfect end to a fabulous trip!

Top and above: Liz gets her hands bound ready for a game of pelota. The losers of the game get big berets to wear – so guess which team Liz was on! Below: Matt taking part in the town's human tower building practice.

Bilbao

Barcelona ●

Madrid **Majorca**

Seville
●

Almeria
●

SUPER FURRY ANIMAL COAT HANGERS

TO MAKE A FURRY COAT HANGER YOU WILL NEED:

- *a plastic coat hanger*
- *fun fur fabric (approx 33 x 60 cm for a dog, a little more for a long-eared rabbit and a little less for a chick)*
- *toy stuffing (kapok) or similar*
- *a button or felt for nose*
- *felt for tongue*
- *paper circles for eyes*
- *ribbon for bow*

1 To make a furry dog coat hanger, cover the main part of the plastic hanger with two strips of fur fabric. Each strip should be about 12 cm

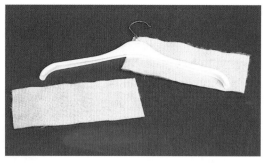

wide and long enough to reach from the hook to the end of the hanger plus a couple of extra centimetres to allow for the seams.

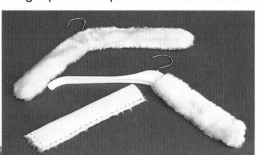

2 Fold the strips in half lengthways, wrong side out, then stitch the long sides of one piece together and one of the short ends. Don't worry if you aren't good at sewing as you don't have to do tiny neat stitches as they will sink into the fur and hardly show.

3 Stitch the second piece in the same way but before you stitch the short end, check that the pile on the fur runs downwards on both strips when seen from the front.

4 Turn the strips furry sides out and slip on to the hanger with the seams at the bottom. Fold in the raw edges a little way and stitch the two strips together.

5 The head is made from two circles of fur. Cut these out using a saucer and a medium sized plate for the patterns. The small circle will be the muzzle. Sew straight stitches around the edge then pull up the thread, leaving a hole in the middle. Over-sew to keep the gathers in place.

6 Use toy stuffing, cotton wool, crumpled kitchen roll or even cut-up (old!) tights to fill the muzzle.

7 The large circle forms the head. Turn over the raw edges of the fur on to the wrong side and sew through both thicknesses. Pull the remaining thread to gather the fabric in the same way as the muzzle. Leave a hole in the middle about 6 cm across.

8 Push the muzzle into this hole, giving it a squeeze if it is a tight fit. You can fix the muzzle to the head with a little glue, but sewing is better.

9 Now fix the head to the hanger. Put a little glue on the front of the hanger beneath the hook. Press the back of the head on to the glue. If the head is wobbly, put on a bit more glue.

10 The ears are made from 12 cm squares of fur. Fold the square in half, fur sides together. Before stitching the ears make sure the fur pile faces downwards on both, so that they will be more realistic to stroke. Now stitch the sides together and sew a pointed

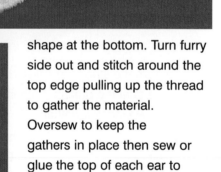

shape at the bottom. Turn furry side out and stitch around the top edge pulling up the thread to gather the material. Oversew to keep the gathers in place then sew or glue the top of each ear to either side of the head.

11 If you use glue to attach the ears, let it dry before putting on the dog's features. You can use a black button for a nose and two black paper circles

make good eyes. A scrap of pink felt makes the tongue. If you pull the fur apart and attach it under the pile, it will look more realistic. A scrap of ribbon tied into a bow will make the furry dog hanger look even more cheerful.

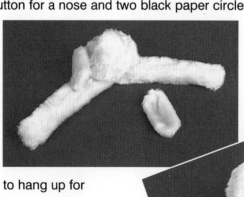

These hangers are cute enough to hang up for fun, let alone using them for clothes. All the creatures have similar shaped faces, but different ears. The long eared rabbit's whiskers are cut from a section of a washing up bottle. Simply cut it into very thin strips.

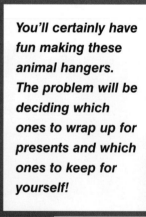

You'll certainly have fun making these animal hangers. The problem will be deciding which ones to wrap up for presents and which ones to keep for yourself!

SIMON ★

LIZ JOINS THE FIREFIGHTERS

LIZ JOINED A GROUP OF RECRUITS AT THE WEST MIDLANDS FIRE SERVICE WHO WERE UNDERGOING A THIRTEEN WEEK INTENSIVE COURSE TO BECOME FIREFIGHTERS

First things first – a thorough lesson in using breathing apparatus

Rolling up the heavy hoses was exhausting.

No problem. Liz gives a perfect fireman's lift.

Liz's first task was a practical one: learning to roll and unroll a hose. Why is it things that look easy never are?

Firefighting is a dangerous job but safety is taken very seriously indeed. Liz learned how to stabilise herself on a ladder and how to give someone a fireman's lift. So far, so good – but could she get dressed on the move?

Boots with trousers already placed around them are ready and waiting to be stepped into. The siren is blaring and the blue light is flashing. Up with the trousers and braces before boarding a fire engine responding to an emergency call. Then it's on with a fireproof balaclava, helmet, jacket and gloves. Breathing apparatus to prevent inhaling poisonous gasses is strapped on her back. It's heavy and cumbersome but nothing compared to what she was about to face – real fire.

Liz is scared even though Station Officer Greg Bowns is her experienced partner. They check each other to make sure no flesh is exposed. Keeping low they enter the blazing house checking all doors for heat before entering. Liz blasts the ceiling with the hose to cool the hot gases. Together Liz and Greg successfully put out a kitchen fire but they're told there's a casualty. The firefighting duo make their way to a blazing bedroom and locate the casualty. They quickly get out of the building.

A successful job done, but of course, it was all a training exercise.

Action stations! The flames were real even though it was a training exercise.

The powerful water jets soon put out the blaze.

Liz was grateful for the experience and full of admiration for the brave men and women who spend four years becoming fully qualified firefighters.

29

hear'say
PURE AND SIMPLE

Ten minutes to transmission and Suzanne puts the final touches to her make-up.

The highlight of the day – meeting Meg!

Danny and Myleene help launch our bikeathon, tandem-style.

When Kym, Suzanne, Myleene, Danny and Noel – otherwise known as Hear'Say – came to the Blue Peter studio they had loads to do. Apart from performing their hit single 'Pure and Simple', they helped cook picnic pasties, compete in the Friday Frenzy and ride bicycles – and they managed to find a few minutes for a quick chat!

KYM

Have you always wanted to be a popstar?
MYLEENE: Always! I went to two classical music schools and shocked them all with my plans! However, they were very supportive.
DANNY: Actually, I always wanted to be a primary school teacher.

Did you ever expect to be picked?
NOEL: I couldn't believe it – I never thought I'd get through each round.
DANNY: I picked all the other guys, but not myself. I was so surprised!
KYM: All through the auditions I never once thought that I was going to get through. So when I found out I was thrilled. I felt like I was flying for about two days.

MYLEENE: We were told to pack for a week of auditions but I took three days' worth of clothes. I didn't want to tempt fate and wasn't too confident either. So as the days went on I ended up shopping after each day.

Since joining the band, what's been the best bit so far?
SUZANNE: It has to be performing at the Brits.
DANNY: … and the record signings when we get to meet all our fans – the support is just amazing.

Any bad times?
NOEL: Only one – having to leave home.
KYM: Yes, it was hard not being able to see my kids regularly. But that's changing now and I see them more often.

How are you coping with the change in your lives?
DANNY: I think we're coping really well – we're on the greatest adventure of our lives.

KYM: We're supporting each other – you could say we're like each others' rocks.

Have you been surprised at all the attention?
NOEL: Absolutely – we never imagined that the show would be such a success.
MYLEENE: After all … we're just five kids that wanted something so badly and got lucky …

DANNY

DANNY: I call it the Big Brother syndrome. I had no idea that 12 million people would be watching our every step.
KYM: But it's great to know we have lots of supporting fans.

Do you think the publicity and success has changed you in any way?
SUZANNE: No, and I hope it never will.
MYLEENE: We probably just look a little more tired!!!

SUZANNE

32

NOEL: I think I've hardened slightly towards cameras but I am still me at heart!

KYM: It's made me stronger and has also made me realise who I can trust under pressure.

What do you do in your spare time?

SUZANNE: What's spare time?!?

NOEL: No, we don't get much – so I tend to sleep!

KYM: And I like to go and see my family (especially my kids) and chill out.

What are your hopes for the future?

NOEL: I just want Hear'Say to be as successful as possible.

DANNY: To keep enjoying this amazing experience and have a successful album.

SUZANNE: And it'd be great to have a Christmas Number 1!

MYLEENE

Does anyone have any annoying habits?

MYLEENE: We all get very tired and silly and spontaneously burst into fits of laughter. I'm sure that annoys anyone around us!

NOEL: Danny farts (it's disgusting!).

DANNY: Hang on, that's what you do…

What's Nasty Nigel really like?

NOEL: He's not really nasty.

MYLEENE: He often comes to the house for dinner and a gossip. He had to play a 'nasty' character for the TV show, but he's really quite friendly and very encouraging.

DANNY: He's cool. I think he told the truth and a lot of people respect that.

And finally … what's your favourite sandwich filling?

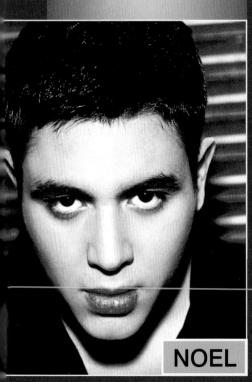

NOEL

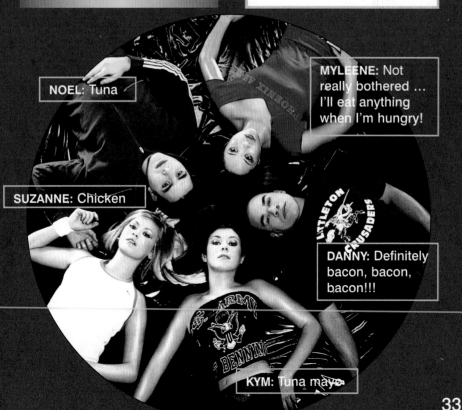

NOEL: Tuna

SUZANNE: Chicken

MYLEENE: Not really bothered … I'll eat anything when I'm hungry!

DANNY: Definitely bacon, bacon, bacon!!!

KYM: Tuna mayo

POMPEII
A CITY FROZEN IN TIME

THIS YEAR SIMON WENT ON THE TRAIL OF EARTHQUAKES AND VOLCANOES. WITH THEIR ENORMOUS NATURAL POWER AND ENERGY THEY HAVE FASCINATED PEOPLE THROUGHOUT HISTORY. HE TRAVELLED TO ITALY IN SEARCH OF ONE PARTICULAR STORY AND FOUND HIMSELF TRAVELLING BACK IN TIME.

Pompeii is an amazing link to the past. As you walk around you get a real sense of what it would have been like to live in a Roman city.

On 24 August in the year AD 79 the world seemed to end for thousands of people living in one of the richest towns in the world.

August had been a fine month. People walked in the streets, shopped in the busy markets and busied themselves in their homes.

The talk was of holidays away from the bustle of Pompeii. Although people had noticed that wells had dried up and small tremors shook buildings from time to time, no one seemed concerned. But on the morning of 20 August people began to worry. Stories were told of the ground appearing to crack in places. Huge waves pounded the shore and, strangest of all, horses in the town and cows in the field grew restless, and birds fled. Although none of them knew it, the townspeople had four days to escape. For those who didn't, 24 August was a day like no other; for many it was their last. For Pompeii it was the end, and the city vanished from history.

Pompeii was a Roman city built in the shadow of Mount Vesuvius. The slopes of the mountain were covered in rich fields and vineyards. Today the volcano is still active but scientists record the activity. Back in AD 79 there was no real warning of what was to come.

For three days the mountain showered fire and ash on the city below. Thousands died. The Roman writer Pliny the Younger left an eye-witness account which speaks of a great cloud, huge flames and the cries of the people trapped. Despite his account, people forgot Pompeii. Farmers in the area worked on the land while ten metres beneath them the Roman city lay undisturbed. But about 250 years ago that changed. When the first archaeologists started to dig they had no idea what to expect. What they found amazed them, as it amazes visitors today.

As Simon saw, Pompeii is a city frozen in time. The buildings have few roofs but the streets are much as they were when Pliny walked along them. Shops, markets and houses all remain standing; all that's missing is the noise and bustle of the living city. Chariots and carts have left their mark in the pavements and you can still walk on the stones placed to stop pedestrians getting their feet muddy! Simon visited the magnificent amphitheatre where gladiators once fought, and read the graffiti written on the walls. He stood at a Roman snack bar and wandered through the deserted forum where the business of the city was carried out. But it's not the great public buildings that make Pompeii such a special place. The homes of the people, rich and poor, offer a very special view of their lives. Today Pompeii is still revealing its secrets after a natural disaster that took place so many centuries ago. "It's difficult to imagine that these streets were once crowded with people running for their lives," said Simon, "until you look up to Mount Vesuvius and wonder whether disaster will ever strike again."

Casts of the bodies of those who died in Pompeii have been made from the marks they left in the ash.

Everything in Pompeii is preserved, from family shrines to beautiful mosaics.

WE THOUGHT IT WAS
TIME TO FIND OUT MORE
ABOUT LIZ AND WHAT
SHE WAS LIKE WHEN SHE
WAS GROWING UP. SO
SHE'S BRAVELY AGREED
TO LET US HAVE A LOOK
THROUGH HER PHOTO
ALBUMS AND TELL US A
BIT ABOUT WHAT SHE
USED TO GET UP TO.

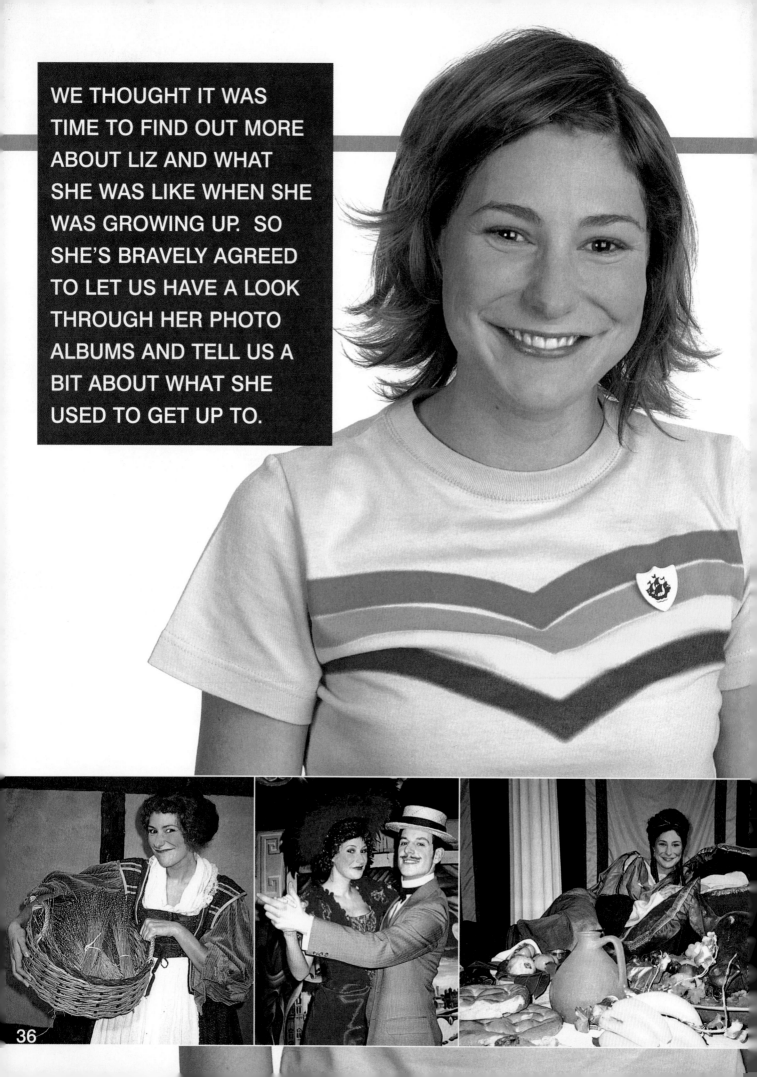

Liz's Scrapbook

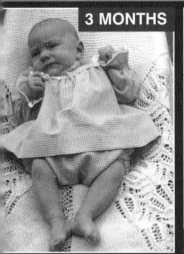
3 MONTHS

6 YEARS

9 YEARS

11 YEARS

19 YEARS

THE EARLY YEARS

Top left: Enjoying one of my favourite hobbies – sleeping!
Top middle: With my younger sister Suzie – I'm the one on the left.
Top right: This is what I looked like at school – as you can see, I was a bit of a tomboy.
Far left: I felt like the cat's whiskers – the purrfect look for a fancy dress party.
Left: Yet another hairdo! This is what I looked like when I was at Southampton University.

I'M HAVING A GREAT TIME BEING A BLUE PETER PRESENTER!

Opposite page (left): Who will buy my sweet blooming lavender? I don't think the dress helped my sales pitch!
Opposite page (middle): Dancing back to days gone by as the star of an East End music hall.
Opposite page (right): As the Lady Barkonius, I was guest of honour at a grand Roman banquet.
Far left: Blasting into the future as Princess Leia, light sabre at the ready.
Left: At the end of a tough day as a trainee firefighter.

37

one-nil!

No matter which team you support, why not re-enact your favourite matches by making your own football game? It's so easy and so much fun you could find yourself playing extra time!

MATERIALS:

- *1 large stackable cardboard fruit box (about 60cm x 35cm)*
- *2 soap powder boxes*
- *thin dowelling or garden canes (enough to make 8 rods)*
- *20 clothes pegs*
- *paint*
- *green card (or paint)*
- *a table tennis ball*
- *glue and coloured sticky tape*

HOW TO MAKE THE MINI TABLE FOOTBALL GAME

The goals are cut from 2 soap powder boxes. You only need part of the boxes so cut all the way round 7 cm from the bottom and then cut away a section on one of the long sides leaving 2 cm on each side.

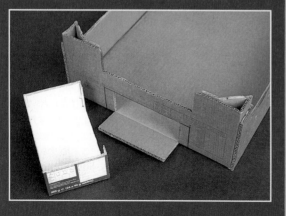

To fit the goal boxes, place each one against the stadium ends, making sure they are in the middle. Draw around them and then draw

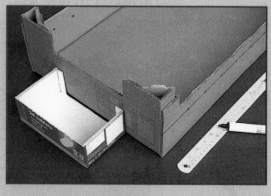

another line 2 cm inside the first and cut along the three sides. You will end up with a fold down flap you can stick your goal box on to.

The rods are 8 lengths of dowel cut 25 cm longer than the width of the stadium. If you need to cut them to size, smooth the ends with sandpaper so you don't get splinters. Put the stadium box on its side and rest a peg on it with its legs on the floor of the box. Make a mark level with the peg hole then make another mark 2 cm above it. Do this at each end and in the middle.

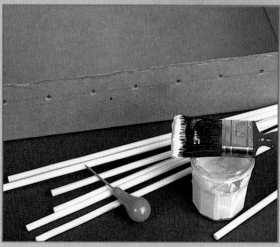

Join up the dots along the top line. Repeat on the other side of the stadium. Now measure and make 8 evenly spaced marks on each of these lines. Carefully use a bradawl to make holes through these marks. Then use a pencil to make the holes big enough for the rods to fit through.

You can paint the stadium box – why not choose your team's colours? When the paint is dry it's time to make the turf. You can either paint the base green or cut out green card to fill the stadium and the goals. Mark the pitch and the goal areas using white paint or white sticky tape.

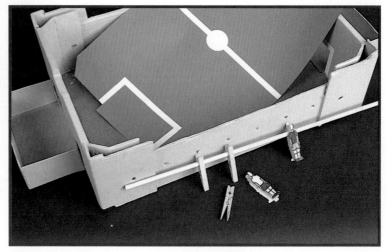

Clip your team into position – the goalies at either end then your defenders and strikers. For extra support you could glue each player to the rods.

To make the teams, draw a simple picture of a player who is about the same size as the pegs. Cut out 40 shapes (you'll need a back and a front for each player). Decide on your team colours and get colouring. You could add tiny photos of your favourite players' faces cut from magazines. If you find the pegs are a little uneven, use sandpaper to level them before sticking your players on using a little glue.

Finally to stop the rods going through the holes wind sticky tape around the ends. If you have two colours alternate them to show which rod controls which team. Use the table tennis ball as a football.

On me 'ead son!

MATT ★

The name's Baker, Matt Baker!

Take me to your leader ...

ANGELS FOR A DAY

Easy, Tiger!

Blue Peter presenters love dressing up so when we sent Matt and Liz to check out the largest and oldest costume store in the world they couldn't resist trying on the odd costume or two!

Angels have been costuming the stars for 160 years and with thousands of outfits to choose from, Matt and Liz were spoilt for choice. They had everything from Cleopatra to the Christmas fairy.

The company began in 1840 as a quality second-hand clothes shop in Covent Garden. In those days actors were expected to provide their own costumes and so they'd come to the shop to rent suitable clothes rather than having to buy them for themselves. These days Angels still make costumes for films, theatre, and television productions – but you don't have to be an actor to wear their outfits as anyone can go along and hire the clothes to wear to a fancy dress party.

Now don't be shy. Do you think they've spotted us?

Kevin Costner actually wore this costume in 'Robin Hood – Prince of Thieves'.

Oooh! It's masked Matt!

This outfit is perfect for clubbing!

Your wish is my command.

Groovy baby.

Just call me Lizzy Spice.

Great outfit for a dinosaur dance.

On guard!

TORTILLA ESPANOLA

IF YOU FANCY GIVING YOUR FAMILY AND FRIENDS A REAL TASTE OF SPAIN THEN THIS IS THE RECIPE FOR YOU. IT'S A TRADITIONAL SPANISH OMELETTE AND YOU CAN SERVE IT FOR BREAKFAST, LUNCH OR TEA. IT'S REALLY FILLING, CAN BE EATEN HOT OR COLD, AND IS SIMPLICITY ITSELF TO MAKE.

INGREDIENTS:
2 large potatoes – peeled and diced
1 onion – chopped
1 green pepper – chopped
1 large tomato (or 2 small ones) – chopped
3 tablespoons olive oil
4 large eggs
salt and pepper to taste

Boil the potato cubes for 8 to 10 minutes, then drain. Heat 3 tablespoons of oil in a non-stick frying pan and add the potato, chopped onion, green pepper and tomato. Stir and cook slowly for about 15 minutes. Crack the eggs into a bowl and whisk. Remove the vegetables from the heat and add to the egg mixture. Stir and season. Now pour the mixture back into the frying pan, adding a little more oil if necessary. Cook for about 5 to 7 minutes, until the bottom of the tortilla is cooked and the top is still a little runny. Remove from the heat. A simple way to cook the top is to grill the tortilla for a few minutes until golden brown. Or put on oven gloves and turn the tortilla over by putting a plate over the frying pan and quickly turning it upside down on to the plate. Then slide the tortilla back into the pan to cook the other side.

How Konnie's trick was done

The secret behind Konnie's magic trick is the glass she used. She'd stuck on to its mouth a piece of paper exactly the same colour as the paper underneath. So the coin is always there – it's just hiding underneath the glass!

If you want to have a go, this is what you do....

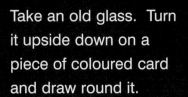

Take an old glass. Turn it upside down on a piece of coloured card and draw round it.

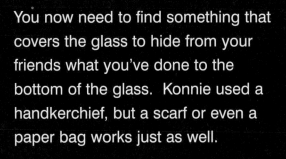

Cut out the circle and stick it to the top edge of the glass. Check that you can't see the join by putting the glass on a piece a paper the same colour as the one you stuck on the top of the glass.

You now need to find something that covers the glass to hide from your friends what you've done to the bottom of the glass. Konnie used a handkerchief, but a scarf or even a paper bag works just as well.

When the cloth is removed it looks as if the coin has disappeared! So clever and so simple!

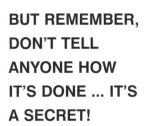

BUT REMEMBER, DON'T TELL ANYONE HOW IT'S DONE ... IT'S A SECRET!

45

JORVIK

Ever heard of Jorvik? Today it is known as York but 1,025 years ago it was Jorvik, a thriving Viking city.

VIKING CITY

JORVIK
THE VIKING CITY

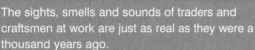
The sights, smells and sounds of traders and craftsmen at work are just as real as they were a thousand years ago.

30 years ago a team of archaeologists found the most detailed evidence of Viking life buried five metres below the modern city streets and in 1984 this became a visitor attraction.

Jorvik has just been redeveloped so that visitors can experience real history as never before. You can see faithful recreations of the Vikings' sophisticated, high-rise buildings, built from oak timbers. They are accurate to the last fence, cess pit and workshop. Archaeological finds like combs (with fossilised head lice still between the teeth!), socks, shoes and rubbish have been put back exactly where they were found.

Who's this canny lad? Looks familiar.

Matt and Mabel enjoy a ride through time.

Dressed in a leotard, work could begin on Matt's body

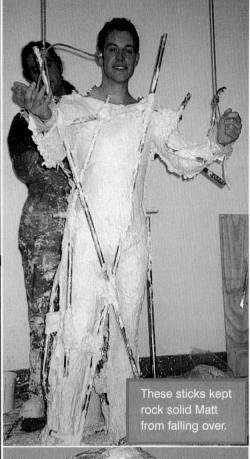

These sticks kept rock solid Matt from falling over.

What about the Vikings themselves? Enter Matt and Mabel. Jorvik is populated with residents modelled on real people. They are perfect in every way and have been painstakingly made by sculptors.

Six months ago Matt met up with the sculptors, Mike and Alistair, who soon had him well and truly plastered. It was just like 'Casualty' as wet bandages were layered on to Matt's body and then covered in plaster of Paris. After half an hour the body cast set solid and each section was carefully removed. The actual model of Matt would be made from fibreglass using the plaster mould.

It was the head next. Matt's hair was covered in polythene and a strip of crumpled foil was laid down the middle so that the mould would come off in two sections. His face and eyes were covered in orange gunge before a layer of plaster was applied. After the mould was removed Matt declared, "It's the worst thing I've ever done for Blue Peter."

Fortunately Mabel didn't have to go through the same process. Using photographs, Mike sculpted Mabel from clay to make a perfect double.

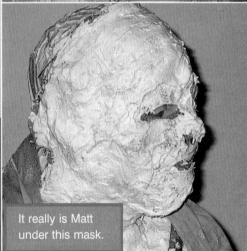

It really is Matt under this mask.

When Jorvik was ready for its re-opening, Matt and Mabel had a sneak preview. They rode back in time seeing, hearing and even smelling the Viking-age city from the River Foss up and over backyards to the street called Coppergate. They stopped off for a close inspection of a couple of familiar faces. Even though the fishmonger had long, blond, Viking hair and blue eyes, there was no mistaking those features. He even wore an ancient Blue Peter badge!

outside broadcast–
BLUE PETER HITS THE ROAD

ONCE A MONTH, THE BLUE PETER TEAM PACKS UP THE STUDIO AND GOES OUT ON THE ROAD. HERE'S WHAT'S INVOLVED IN GETTING ONE OF THESE OUTSIDE BROADCASTS OR OBS UP AND RUNNING.

When we heard that an outdoor ice rink was being built at Somerset House in London, it sounded like the perfect location for our Christmas OB.

Work begins at about 8 o'clock in the morning when the two OB vans turn up. One contains all the equipment, and the other's the scanner, which is where the director sits, along with the production assistant, producer, engineer and sound supervisor.

8.00am: Equipment is unloaded and the crew starts rigging the cameras.

8.30am: The OB van gets set up.

9.00am: Staging is put in place.

9.30am: Carol the camera supervisor finishes cabling.

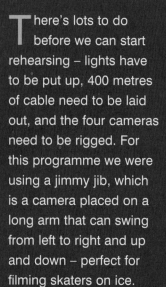

There's lots to do before we can start rehearsing – lights have to be put up, 400 metres of cable need to be laid out, and the four cameras need to be rigged. For this programme we were using a jimmy jib, which is a camera placed on a long arm that can swing from left to right and up and down – perfect for filming skaters on ice.

48

10.00am: Planning meeting begins.

11.00am: Time to rehearse with cameras.

Two hours later and everything is in place. The director, Adrian, has a quick planning meeting to explain where each item is going to take place and where the presenters will stand. Then he heads off to the scanner where he puts on a headset microphone so that everyone can hear what he has to say through their headphones or 'cans'. The first thing to rehearse is the opening of the show. While Adrian talks through the type of shots he wants, the floor manager, Simone, shows Konnie, Simon and Matt where they need to skate to say their lines. It's been a long time since the team had been on ice, but after a couple of rehearsals everyone is happy and it's time to move on.

There's plenty to rehearse – two dance numbers on the ice, appeal news, and a Christmas make.

2.00pm: Simon discusses positions with the floor manager.

3.00pm: Final rehearsal of appeal news.

5.00pm: On air!

During the day the producer, Richard, watches on an outside monitor and uses a walkie-talkie to speak to Adrian if he wants any changes. Timings are crucial, and the PA, Lucy, uses a stopwatch to time each item so that the programme isn't too long or too short.

Before we know it, it's nearly 5 o'clock. Everyone goes to their opening positions – this is it, there's no going back now. Five, four, three, two, one – we're on air.

The Blue Peter
MILLENNIUM CROWN

The Crown Jewels are displayed in the Jewel House at the Tower of London and represent hundreds of years of English history. Most of the collection dates from the restoration of the monarchy in 1660, when Charles II ascended the throne. The last crowns to be added were made for the coronation in 1937. That is, until Blue Peter viewers were asked to design a 21st century crown for the Tower of London.

20,620 designs came flooding in featuring a fantastic variety of ideas ranging from London landmarks, the planets and space travel, the Union Jack, the figures 2000 and the letters MM.

The overall winner was 11-year-old Georgina Elliott from Cheam in Surrey, who designed a Millennium Hedgerow Crown. A dedicated team of craftsmen at Asprey & Garrard spent over 500 hours working by hand to reproduce Georgina's work as an actual crown.

HEDGEROW CROWN

Gold ears of wheat studded with diamonds.

Leaves and grasses made from gold, platinum and silver.

Blackberries made from Amethysts and Garnets.

Rosehips coloured with enamel.

Green Velvet (to represent the meadow).

Hawthorn Berries encrusted with rubies.

The Governor of the Tower of London and the Crown Jeweller, together with Konnie and Liz, had a tough job judging the entries as the standard was so high.

Some of the other winners

Krystal Fox aged 6

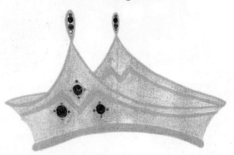

Nicola Milton aged 12

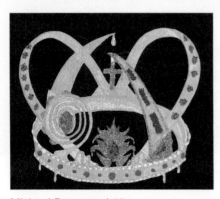

Michael Dato aged 13

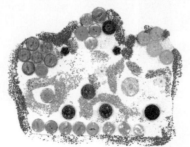

Megan Gee aged 5

Robyn Bennett aged 10

50

THE MAKING OF THE MILLENNIUM CROWN

Craftsmen made a solid silver base from which the individual flowers and grasses would grow.

Flowers and berries were made and mounted into the crown, around a central ear of corn.

Diamonds were set by hand into each ear of corn.

Each blackberry, rosehip and thistle was individually made and set with rubies, amethysts or enamel as shown in Georgina's drawing.

With the flowers and berries in place, each blade of grass was individually made and satin finished in strengthening sterling silver before being placed on the crown.

A deep band of green cushioned velvet was hand sewn and attached to the crown to represent the meadow.

The Millennium Crown was complete and on 30 March 2001 Georgina, together with David Thomas, the Crown Jeweller, was invited to officially hand it over to the Tower, where it has been put on permanent display for millions of visitors from all over the world to admire.

starry starry night

When Blue Peter astronomer Anton Vamplew invited Konnie to take a look around Britain's biggest telescope, she jumped at the chance – but it wasn't as close to home as she'd imagined!

Above: Anton and Konnie in front of the William Herschel telescope – Britain's biggest telescope!
Below: One of the Hegra Atmospheric Cherenkov Telescopes.

The telecope is on the Spanish island of La Palma, which lies off the west coast of Africa. At the centre of the island lies the world's largest volcanic crater – it's about 28 kilometres around the edge, and over 700 metres deep.

At the island's highest point, which is 2,400 metres above sea level, is the **Roque de los Muchachos Observatory.** It's way above the clouds, so conditions are perfect for star-spotting because it's above the main part of the atmosphere. The skies are clear and it's far enough away from any major towns or cities to avoid light pollution.

The observatory is home to Britain's biggest telescope – **the William Herschel Telescope** – named after the British astronomer who is best remembered for his discovery of the planet Uranus in 1781.

The astronomical telescope weighs about 210 tonnes – and it has been used to gaze at all sorts of stars in the deepest, darkest regions of the universe. Anton explained that you don't actually look through a telescope like this one.

Instead, there are lots of different electronic instruments which collect information which is then sent to the control room where it is analysed by computers.

Once the telescope had been lowered into position, Konnie noticed the most important part of it – its huge mirror, which measures 4.2 metres across and is 60 cm thick. Anton also showed Konnie the Swedish Solar Tower, which is where astronomers study the sun. This is the earth's nearest star (a mere 93 million miles away!) and it's one of the smallest. You should never look at the sun through a telescope or binoculars as it can do your eyes some serious damage.

Anton told Konnie about sunspots, which are cooler regions on the sun about the size of the earth, or even larger. The more sunspots there are, the more active the sun is. And the more active the sun is, the more flares and material is sent out into space. If this stuff reaches earth, it can cause power cuts or satellite communications to malfunction. But it's not all bad news because they also give us some marvellous sights in the night skies known as the Northern and Southern Lights.

Once the sun had set, the stars came out; Konnie had never seen so many. The perfect end to a perfect day!

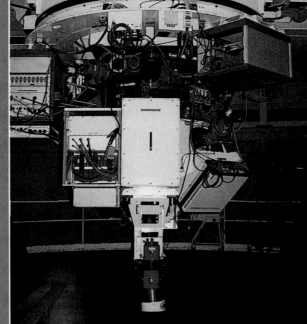

This is what it looks like from the outside.

Three different parts of the William Herschel Telescope. Top: this shows all the electronic instruments used to collect information. Middle: the massive mirror. Bottom: the upper half of the telescope.

APPLE LAYER CAKE

Is it a cake or is it a pud? Actually, it's both!

Preheat the oven to 180°C or gas mark 4.
- Separate the yolks and whites of 6 eggs and whisk the whites until they form peaks.
- Add the sugar in two halves. Beat the first half into the egg whites then use a large metal spoon to gently fold in the rest.
- Grate the yellow skin of the lemon finely.
- Beat the egg yolks with a fork then add the lemon zest. Fold the yolk mixture into the whites.
- Sift the flour and fold in a little at a time. Add the melted butter then stir everything together.
- Grease a 20 cm diameter round cake tin and dust lightly with flour. Put just less than half the mixture in the cake tin and pop it in the oven for about 10 minutes until this layer has set slightly.
- While the first layer is cooking, peel, core and slice 2 cooking apples. Take the cake tin out of the oven and carefully spread the apple slices over the first layer. Now pour on the rest of the mixture to make the final layer.

- Put the cake back in the oven for about 45 minutes. When it's ready the cake should be brown and slightly shrunk away from the sides of the tin. A handy tip for testing is to pop a skewer into the middle and if it comes out clean, the cake is done.

Leave the cake to stand for 5 minutes before turning out on to a cooling rack. Our Apple Layer Cake can be eaten hot or cold and is delicious served with custard or cream.

Dear
Blue Peter

Keep those letters and photos coming. We love hearing from you and decorating our office notice board with your pictures. There's also a chance they might get shown on the programme or end up in our book!

SANTA'S SLEIGH

This is a picture of the reindeer and sleigh that you made and I filled them with chocolates. I really enjoyed making it, it looked lovely on the table on Christmas day.

Hannah (aged 9)
Auckley, Doncaster

TASTY TRAIN TREAT

This is a picture of me and my cousin Darryl making Simon's train cake – we really enjoyed making it and it tasted pretty good too!

Jamie (aged 10) and Darryl (aged 12) Bridge of Allen, Stirling

FESTIVE FLOWERS

This is a photo of me with my Christmas decoration that I saw on your programme. I loved the idea so I copied it but in my own style. I love the show – it's fab!

Jessica (aged 9)
Sompting, West Sussex

COOL COOKIES

This is me and my sister with our Catherine Wheel cookies. They were really fun to make and a lot of effort was needed to stir the mixture but they were very tasty!

Heledd (aged 11) and Llinos (aged 8) Glyneath, South Wales

SPOTTY DOG

I watched you make animals from hangers and this is a picture of the dalmatian that I made. Isn't he lovely!

Alice (aged 5) Hertford

MAKES ARE F.A.B.

This is me painting my Tracy Island, and the finished one. I really enjoyed making it and I did it on my own Workmate. I like doing all your makes, they are really fun!

Adam (aged 9)
Downend, Bristol

BEDS FOR BARBIE

I saw the programme where you made the Barbie bunk beds and decided to make them too. When I had finished them my baby dolls looked left out so I made a cot as well. I used cocktail sticks for the bars and used your ideas for the mattress and cover.

Alice (aged 9) Norwich, Norfolk

PARTY CAKE

Here is a picture of me and my friends eating the train cake at my birthday party. I made the cake myself and it was DELICIOUS!

Robin (aged 10)
Liverpool

THE LOWDOWN ON BLUE PETER BADGES

Blue Peter badges are special because we don't give them away – they have to be won, and worn with pride. We don't even mind upsetting VIPs who ask for badges for their children – the answer will always be, sorry, but no!

Since the Blue badge was introduced in 1962, our collection has grown to five. Here's how you can win one and become part of our huge family of badge holders.

BLUE badges are what the presenters usually wear. You could win one by sending us an interesting letter, giving us a good idea, a tasty recipe, a picture, poem or story. If you ever take part in the programme, this is the badge you'll be awarded.

SILVER badges are awarded to viewers who have already won a Blue badge – but you have to do something different to win one! If you won your Blue badge by sending us a really good drawing, you could invent a recipe for us to try to win your Silver.

GREEN badges are our environmental awards. If you tell us about an environmental project, write a poem, a song or give us your views about any 'green' subject, you could win a Green badge. Let us know what you have been doing to help the world around you.

COMPETITION badges are awarded to winners and runners up. We always have lots of competitions on the programme so you have more chances than you might think of winning one.

GOLD badges are our highest award. They are very rare and are awarded to people for outstanding bravery and courage or for representing your country in an international event. You can't 'earn' a Gold badge by winning all the others. Recent Gold awards have been made to the first Children's Laureate, the writer and artist Quentin Blake, to tennis ace Greg Rusedski and to one of the first women to reach the South Pole, Catherine Hartley.

BLUE BADGE – for writing in or taking part in the programme

SILVER BADGE – if you've already won a Blue!

GOLD BADGE – our top award for bravery or courage

GREEN BADGE – our environmental award

COMPETITION BADGE – for winners and runners up

There are TREATS for Blue Peter badge holders. They entitle you to free entry at over 200 attractions all over the UK. When you win a badge, we'll send you a list of all these places. You must wear your badge when you visit one, though. And by the way, if your Mum or Dad won a badge when they were young, tell them that, sadly, free entry only counts for viewers under 16!

59

GO 4 FREE –

THAT'S IF YOU'VE WON YOUR BLUE PETER BADGE!

When we're filming around the UK at places we think you'd enjoy, we always ask if viewers can have free entry. New attractions are always being added to the list and here are just a few great places you should try.

THE EDEN PROJECT

The Eden Project is a giant global garden built in a huge china clay pit the size of 35 football pitches. Two enormous conservatories house plants from all over the world. You can go on an adventure into the crater and get the feeling you're in a real rainforest. Don't miss it if you are anywhere near St Austell in Cornwall.

THE BRONTË PARSONAGE

The Brontës were an extraordinary literary family and the Parsonage at Haworth was their lifelong home. It's near Keighley on the edge of the Yorkshire moors and is full of the Brontës' furniture and possessions, bringing the rooms to life just as they would have been when the family lived there. The Parsonage houses a unique collection of treasures including the 'little books' the Brontës produced as children and which Liz saw when she visited. It's incredible to think that Charlotte, Branwell, Emily and Anne wrote some of the greatest novels in the English language while they lived here.

JORVIK

If you want to time travel back to the time of the Vikings, make a beeline for Jorvik in the famous city of York. It's just had a face-lift and is filled with sights, sounds and smells from centuries ago. Keep your eyes peeled for two familiar Blue Peter faces!

THE TOWER OF LONDON

This has to be the most spectacular landmark of London. The Tower of London was begun by William the Conqueror in 1078 and has 900 years of Royal history behind its gates. Yeoman Warders – popularly known as Beefeaters – have guarded this fortress for centuries and will give you a tour. You can marvel at the Crown Jewels and don't miss their latest acquisition – a Millennium Crown designed by a Blue Peter competition winner.

Check our website for a full list and always phone to check opening times before making a special trip.

WIN A DAY AT THE BLUE PETER STUDIO!

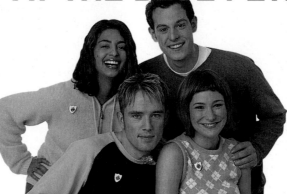

The winner, with friend and family (maximum 4 persons), will be invited to the Blue Peter studio to meet members of the team. The winner's transport costs to London will be provided.

Simply answer this question and you're in with a chance!

Where is Britain's largest telescope?

- Competition entries must be received by 1 February 2002.
- Venue and visit date will be agreed with the winner.
- The winner will be notified by post no later than 1 March 2002.
- Send your answer, along with your name, age and address to: Blue Peter Competition, Egmont World, Unit 7, Millbank House, Riverside Park, Bollin Walk, Wilmslow, Cheshire SK9 1BJ.
- Remember! Competition closing date is 1 February 2002.

RULES
1 Entrants must be under 16 years of age.
2 One winner will be chosen at random and notified by post.
3 The judges' decision will be final. No correspondence can be entered into.
4 Employees (and their relatives) of Egmont World and their associated companies are not eligible to enter.
5 Entries are limited to one per person.
6 The competition is open to residents of the UK, Ireland and the Channel Islands.
7 The publishers reserve the right to vary the prizes, subject to availability.

Our address is: Blue Peter, BBC, London W12 7RJ
Our home page is: http://www.bbc.co.uk/bluepeter
e-mail:bluepeter@bbc.co.uk

Furry Animal Coat Hangers (pp 24–26)
and Table Football (pp 38–40) by Margaret Parnell
Food (pp 44 and 54) by Gillian Shearing

PHOTOGRAPHIC ACKNOWLEDGEMENTS
Apex Photography p 60 (top left)
Asprey & Garrard p 51
Mike Baker, p 14 (top left and right)
Chris Capstick, pp 30–31, 50 (top right), 51 (bottom right)
Kim Cessford Studio, p 16 (top right)
Luke Finn, pp 48–49
Martyn Goddard, pp 12–13, 15 (bottom), 24–26, 38–40, 45, 54,
58–59, 62–63
Marylin Kingwill, p 48 (top right)
Gary Moyes, pp 2–3, 27, 41, 44, 55
Polydor Records pp 32–33
Paul Sweeney pp 16–17
Anton Vamplew pp 52–53
West Midlands Fire Service pp 28-–29
Yorkshire Evening Post p 47 (bottom left and right)

All other photographs are © Blue Peter and were taken by Richard
Marson, Bridget Caldwell, Emma Clark, Moray London, Joanna
Robinson and lots of Blue Peter viewers. If we have left anyone
out we're sorry. The authors would like to specially thank Clare
Eades, and the whole Blue Peter team for their help and ideas.

Every effort has been made to contact the copyright holders for
permission to reproduce material in this book. If any material has
been included without permission please contact the publisher.